The Light Between Oceans: A Guide for Book Clubs

KATHRYN COPE

CONTENTS

1 - INTRODUCTION

The Reading Room Book Group Guides

This is one of a series of guides designed to make your book group meetings more dynamic and engaging. Packed with information, the Reading Room Book Group Guides are an invaluable resource to ensure that your discussions never run dry.

How you choose to use the guides is entirely up to you. The 'Author Biography', 'Historical Context' and 'Literary Style' sections provide useful background information which may be interesting to share with your group at the beginning of your meeting. The all-important list of discussion questions, which will probably form the core of your meeting, can be found in Chapter 10. To support your responses to the discussion questions, you may find it helpful to refer to the 'Themes and Symbols' and 'Character Analysis' sections.

A plot synopsis is provided as an aide-memoire to recap on the finer points of the plot and clarify the precise sequence of events in the novel. There is also a quick quiz - a fun way to bring your discussion to a close. Finally, if this was a book that you particularly enjoyed, either as a group or as an individual, the guide concludes with a list of books similar in either style or subject matter.

Be warned, this guide contains spoilers. Please do not be tempted to read it before you have read the original book as plot surprises will be well and truly ruined.

2 – WHY READ *THE LIGHT BETWEEN OCEANS?*

M.L. Stedman's *The Light Between Oceans* is one of those rare books that succeeds in straddling the boundaries between popular and literary fiction. An international bestseller, its movie rights have already been snapped up by DreamWorks. It has also received literary acclaim, winning three prestigious Australian Book Industry Awards and being longlisted for the Women's Prize for Fiction.

The central premise behind the plot of Stedman's novel is immediately gripping: Isabel and Tom, a couple who live alone on an island, long for a child and one day, a baby girl drifts ashore in a boat. The baby's father, also in the boat, is dead. Is this mysterious event the miracle they have been praying for? Should the couple keep the baby, as Isabel suggests? These questions alone would be sufficient to provide all the ingredients for a page turning novel; which *The Light Between Oceans* undoubtedly is. There is also a richness and complexity to this story which far surpasses the remit of most commercial fiction.

Stedman writes beautifully. Her vivid prose captures both the beauty and the savagery of the Australian landscape. Janus Lighthouse, the striking central image of the novel, serves as a metaphor for several opposing themes: light and darkness, safety and danger, isolation and communication. The rendering of historical period in the novel is also exceptionally well-executed. Setting the action in the mid-to late 1920s, Stedman succeeds in conveying the collective sense of shock and loss experienced by communities following World War I. She also thoughtfully explores the universal themes of love, loss, morality and the redemptive power of forgiveness.

The complexity of the characters and the enormity of the decisions that they face makes the novel an absolute gift for reading groups. The complex moral dilemmas Stedman presents invite us to put ourselves in the place of the characters and decide if we would take the same action in their shoes. Few readers will be able to complete *The Light Between Oceans* without forming strong opinions about the 'rights and wrongs' of the characters' actions. Some will love the way Isabel is compelled to follow the instincts of her heart while others will find her selfish. Many will admire Tom's selflessness, while others will find his preoccupation with following rules irritating. One thing is guaranteed – any group discussion will prove lively and entertaining.

3 – M.L. STEDMAN

M. L. Stedman is a writer who shuns the limelight. She has given away little biographical information in her few media interviews, believing that her personal life has little relevance to her work as an author. This belief is reflected in her decision to use only her initials in her authorial name (her first name is Margot).

The landscape of *The Light Between Oceans* was inspired by Stedman's memories of her childhood in Perth, Western Australia. As an adult, she moved to London where she worked as a lawyer.

Stedman's writing career began when she made the decision to hire a writing coach and embarked on a creative writing holiday in Greece. *The Light Between Oceans* began as a short story, which her agent encouraged her to develop into a novel. The final manuscript was subject to a bidding war between publishers and the novel has now been published in over 30 territories.

4 – LITERARY STYLE

Stedman's prose is lyrical and poetic. She writes from a third person perspective, allowing the reader to access the thoughts of not only the central characters of Tom, Isabel and Hannah but also the more minor characters whose lives are all touched by Tom's and Isabel's actions.

LETTERS

The narrative of *The Light Between Oceans* is interspersed with letters, which play a crucial role in plot development and in revealing the state of mind of certain characters.

Letters are an essential communication tool between Janus Island and the mainland. They also inform relatives of the deaths of their loved ones during the war and even allow characters to speak after their deaths (e.g. Edward Sherbourne's letter to Tom and Isabel's letter to Lucy-Grace).

Letters offer a way for characters to reach out to one another in the novel. It is Isabel's first letter to Tom which sows the seeds of their romance. Isabel's decision not to write to her parents after her baby is stillborn becomes a crucial omission of communication as it allows her to pass Lucy off as her own and marks the beginning of the many deceits that will follow. Significantly, it is the letter Tom writes to Isabel from the police cells that finally reminds her of how much she loves him. Isabel's initial reluctance to read the letter demonstrates that she is aware of the power his words will have on her and the painful sacrifice she will have to make as a consequence.

5 – HISTORICAL CONTEXT

AUSTRALIA & WORLD WAR I

Although *The Light Between Oceans* is set in the period following World War I, its presence is still very much felt. Stedman examines the aftermath of the Great War, demonstrating the way it has scarred Tom psychologically and also the way it has affected the Australian citizens' sense of nationalism.

The Great War is viewed as a crucial period of history in shaping Australia's sense of national identity. Prior to WWI, the majority of Australians thought of themselves as 'Australasian Britons': an offshoot of the British empire. When war was declared, Australia demonstrated its loyalty to the British empire, willingly joining with the Allied forces and sending over 320,000 of its men to fight. The Australian Imperial Force (AIF) were first sent to Egypt and then on to invade the Greek peninsula of Gallipoli in 1915 in a strategic attempt to capture Constantinople. The AIF also served on the Western front from 1916 to 1918 and fought on the Somme in 1916.

The war had great significance for Australians as it was the first major military conflict they took part in as an independent nation. Its effects were twofold: Australia gained a new sense of national pride but at the expense of losing many of its men.

On landing at Anzac Cove in Gallipoli, Australian soldiers (along with New Zealanders) were surprised to find that, although less experienced in warfare, they were more efficient than the largely disorganised British troops. The battle at Gallipoli was bloody and protracted. The troops were finally withdrawn after eight months of hard fighting and the episode was considered an Allied failure. On the Somme, as many men were lost in a week as had been killed during eight months on Gallipoli. Many Australian soldiers became increasingly resentful as, although they were serving the empire, they were made to feel different from the British troops.

The combination of grief over lost men, increasing resentment of the British and the discovery that they were skilled soldiers as a nation, led to an emerging sense of nationalism for Australian citizens. This feeling created the 'Anzac legend': a celebration of the toughness and resilience of the Australian soldier, echoing the self-reliant and practical nature of the original Australian bushman. Rather than being just another part of the British empire, Australians now felt they had a clear identity that they could take pride in. The date of the Anzac Cove landing, 25th April, became known as 'Anzac Day' and it remains the most significant military commemoration for Australians and New Zealanders.

In Stedman's novel, the aftermath of all these elements upon the residents of Point Partaguese is explored. There is a tangible sense of loss in the community as few families have been left untouched by tragedy. The Graysmarks have lost both of their sons who were fighting together on the Somme. It is unsurprising, therefore, that Tom feels guilty about surviving when so many of his compatriots did not return home. He also refuses to take pride in his efficiency as a soldier, despite having received military honours.

The town's strong sense of nationalism is also evident. On their celebration of Anzac Day, the residents are stirred to a fever pitch of national pride heavily tinged with grief and anger. Stedman demonstrates how easily nationalism can tip over into xenophobia and racism when the generally well-behaved citizens of Partaguese hound Frank literally to his death. As the 'foreigner' of the community, Frank becomes the scapegoat for the town's complex and unresolved emotions about the war.

6 - THEMES & SYMBOLS

LIGHT

As the novel's title suggests, light is a recurring symbol in *The Light Between Oceans*. The image of the lighthouse on Janus Island pervades the novel and the light it casts out is associated with safety. On a practical level, the purpose of the beam of the lighthouse is to ensure the safety of passing ships. Tom is attracted to the job of lighthouse keeper as he sees it as an opportunity to save lives after being forced to take the lives of other men in the war. Tom's meticulous care of the working parts of the lighthouse and his daily lighting of it almost take on the significance of religious ritual, demonstrating how seriously he takes the role. For Isabel, after the arrival of the baby, the light's reassuring hum and glow seems to confirm the sensation that they are safe from the reach of the real world there. Her decision to call the baby Lucy, meaning light, illustrates not only the joy the child brings into their lives, but also a determination to keep her safe.

Ironically, while the lighthouse casts its beam thirty miles out to sea, it leaves Janus Island in darkness. This reflects the moral darkness that Isabel and Tom venture into when they decide to keep the child. It also foreshadows the fact that the safety the island offers to them is an illusion.

THE OCEAN

Surrounding the lighthouse are two oceans. On one side of the island is the Indian Ocean, which is warm and inviting. On the other side is the treacherous Southern Ocean which harbours an angry energy. The fact that these two such disparate bodies of water merge at some imperceptible point underlines one of the messages of the novel - that nothing can be defined by one quality alone. Light can signal danger as well as safety, love can lead to hatred and questions of right and wrong are rarely clearly delineated.

LOVE

Tom and Isabel's love for each other is central to the plot of the novel. Although Tom has attempted to close off his heart after his experiences in the war, when he meets Isabel he finds there is something about her that breaks down his emotional barriers. Theirs is one of several loving marriages depicted in the novel (there is also Hannah and Frank, Bill and Violet, and Ralph and Hilda).

In some instances, however, love is shown to make the characters behave badly or against their own belief systems. It is Tom's overwhelming love for Isabel which leads him to agree to keep the baby, even though the decision greatly troubles his conscience. Similarly, Isabel's overpowering love for Lucy leads her to knowingly deprive another woman of her child. It also turns her against Tom, who she almost allows to be tried for murder, as a punishment for his role in their loss of Lucy.

Tom, whose love for Isabel remains unchanged, struggles to comprehend how love can become so distorted. Prepared to face death to protect his wife, he lives in hope that her love for him will at some point be restored.

Isabel's conflict between her love for her husband and her love for Lucy raises the question of whether maternal love is more powerful than romantic love.

MOTHERHOOD

Many of the characters in the novel lose their mothers when they are children – namely, Tom, Hannah and Gwen, Septimus and Frank. There are also several mothers who lose their children (Isabel, Hannah, Violet and Sergeant Knuckey's wife).

Although parental love is explored generally, the bond between mother and child is depicted as being particularly strong. The loss of a child is a tragedy that a woman never recovers from and Isabel's actions are placed within this context. Very early in their relationship, Isabel tells Tom that she wants lots of children. The urge to have and love a child is so strong for her that she is prepared to take another woman's, knowing the suffering this will cause.

Tom knows from his own experience that children need the nurturing influence of a mother. Ironically, Lucy-Grace, who appears to have no mother at the start of the novel, acquires two mothers. The conflict this causes proves almost as traumatic as being motherless. The opposing claims

Isabel and Hannah feel they have over Lucy-Grace raises interesting questions about motherhood. Although Isabel has no right to call herself the child's mother, does she earn this through the love and care she invests in her? At the end of the novel, Lucy-Grace tells Tom that becoming a mother herself has helped her understand the viewpoints of both Hannah and Isabel. Now that she has a son of her own, she would do anything to protect him.

LOSS

The pain caused by loss is a recurrent theme through the novel. Set against the collective grief experienced by the residents of Partaguese as a result of the war, are the details of individual losses, e.g. the deaths of Hugh and Alfie Graysmark, and Tom's separation from his mother when he was a boy.

The lighthouse keeper who precedes Tom on Janus Island is a cautionary example of the devastating effects of loss. Unable to cope with the death of his wife, he loses his mind and eventually ends his own life by jumping off a cliff. Isabel experiences a different but comparable desperation over the loss of her babies. Hannah grieves the loss of her husband and baby and once she is reunited with Grace, mourns the years of her daughter's childhood that she has been deprived of. As Tom comes to realise, the scars that loss leaves are a painful but inevitable part of life and we can either let them destroy us or accept them.

INSTINCT VERSUS RULES

Throughout the novel there is an ongoing battle between the observance of rules and the following of instinct. These two apparently opposing philosophies are embodied in the characters of Tom and Isabel.

After the bloodshed he has witnessed in the war, Tom is a firm believer in following rules. He has learned from experience that in an environment where men are not only allowed but expected to kill their fellow human beings, the usual moral standards no longer apply. In his eyes, adherence to wartime regulations was the only thing that prevented men from turning into inhumane monsters. When Tom becomes a lightkeeper, he finds a certain reassurance in the dictatorial '*Instructions to Lightkeepers*' manual, as he feels adhering to them prevents him from wandering into a moral no man's land. He is soothed by the ritual of inspecting and maintaining his surroundings.

Into this orderly environment comes Isabel, who delights in breaking rules and believes in following her heart. Her idea that they make love at Tom's workstation in the lighthouse is an example of this, as is her short experiment with naturism. Whilst Tom resists these smaller rebellions (carrying her back down the stairs to make love, and insisting that the wearing of clothes is actually far more practical), he caves in to Isabel on her most significant contravention of 'rules', allowing her to keep the baby. Tom's guilt over this transgression of moral rules is shown in his fretting over the log book. He continually flicks back to the blank space he has left in it, where the discovery of the baby and her dead father should have been recorded.

As far as Isabel is concerned, love is far more important than rules and regulations. Although she is aware that she and Tom have committed a number of crimes, (including child abduction and failing to report a dead body), she never waivers in her belief that her love for the child overrules the law. When Tom questions this, she accuses him of loving rules more than his family.

DIVISIONS & LABELLING

When Isabel annotates the map of Janus Island with her own place names, (i.e. 'Tom's Lookout', 'Izzy's Cliff'), her husband is highly uncomfortable with the results. At first this seems like another, rather comic, example of Tom's dislike of flouting lightkeeper regulations. We discover, however, that part of his unease stems from the dangers he sees in dividing and labelling things. When Tom surveys the landscape from the lighthouse, he sees endless space. This boundlessness only confirms his belief that men's desire to fight over patches of land in order to label them as their own is essentially futile. Tom is content to feel he is a part of the island, without ever feeling the need to own or label it.

The insidious consequences of labelling and dividing things can be seen in the treatment of Frank by the residents of Partaguese. Although he is Austrian, he is labelled a 'Hun' and 'as good as' German, turning him into the scapegoat for the town's collective grief over the war.

FAITH & PRAYER

Faith plays a large part in the lives of the characters in the novel. They pray to God for help, guidance, strength and forgiveness at moments when they feel adrift in their lives.

God's hand is seen by the characters to be behind every major event in the novel. When the baby lands on Janus Island, Isabel chooses to believe that her prayers have been answered and that the child is a gift from God. This notion has been planted in Isabel's mind by Violet Graysmark who tells her to keep praying for babies and if God wills it, they will arrive. The belief that God can bestow miracles is also highlighted in the reaction of the residents of Partaguese when Hannah's child is returned to her. Suddenly, there is a noticeable increase of female worshippers at church, all praying to St Jude for their own lost children, who will clearly never return.

The will of God is often used in the novel as an excuse for inexcusable actions. Although deep down Isabel knows that she is wrong to keep the baby, particularly when she discovers the mother is still alive, she convinces herself that God wishes her to keep Lucy. Similarly, the inhabitants of Partaguese gloss over their own shameful role in Frank's disappearance and suggest that his tragic end was a sign of God's disapproval.

Hannah's genuine religious faith is demonstrated when Lucy-Grace goes missing and she makes a silent pact with God. Although she could easily renege on her promise to give the child back to Isabel, she is prepared to honour it, despite the pain it causes her.

FORGIVENESS

Throughout the novel, several of the characters have to make the choice between forgiveness and punishment. Punishment is demonstrated to be the easiest outlet for pain and distress. Isabel chooses to punish Tom for her loss of Lucy, Hannah is tempted to punish the Sherbournes for stealing her child and Frank is punished by the community for the sins of an entire nation. As the characters discover, however, after the urge to lash out is sated, punishment of others provides little satisfaction or resolution.

Forgiveness, on the other hand, is presented as a redemptive force which allows the giver to move on with their lives. Both Tom and Frank are naturally forgiving of others, despite the hardships they face, whilst Isabel and Hannah embark on journeys where they will learn to forgive by the end. Only when Isabel forgives Tom can she admit her own responsibility for events and go on to heal their marriage. Similarly, Hannah has to forgive the Sherbournes before she can make a new start with her daughter. When Lucy-Grace forgives Tom and Isabel for their actions at the end of the novel, it demonstrates that she has learned from the experience of both of her mothers and is not prepared to waste her life in bitterness and resentment.

7 - LOCATION

Point Partaguese

Partaguese is a fictional coastal town in West Australia. Stedman describes in the novel how the town's sense of identity is changed by the war. Previously a self-sufficient but relatively isolated community, the inhabitants felt untouched by the rest of the world. Once World War I commenced, however, its men went to war along with the rest of the nation. When the novel begins, the town is still in shock from the war's impact. Many of its men were lost or, if they returned, it was with something integral 'missing' (either their limbs or their wits). It is the town's collective sense of grief and anger that leads to their shameful treatment of Frank.

Janus Island

Those wishing to visit Janus after reading *The Light Between Oceans* will be disappointed to learn that the island with the lighthouse is also a creation of the author's imagination. Surrounded by the warm Indian Ocean on one side and the savage Southern Ocean on the other, it lies almost 100 miles away from the Australian mainland. A square mile in size, it is home to only the Sherbournes, some sheep and a few goats and chickens. It is a beautiful but savage place which is battered by winds and the ocean.

The isolation of the island is crucial to Stedman's plot, as it is only this that makes it possible for the Sherbournes to pass Lucy off as their own child. It also has a bearing on the moral judgements Isabel makes, as their distance from the rest of the world causes her to erroneously feel that they can escape its value systems.

8 - PLOT SYNOPSIS

PART I

The novel opens on 27th April 1926. Married couple, Isabel and Tom Sherbourne, are the only occupants of Janus Island which lies roughly 100 miles away from the Australian mainland. Isabel is attending the grave of her stillborn baby when she hears a baby's cry. Tom also hears the sound and discovers that a dinghy has drifted to shore. The Sherbournes are astonished to find the dinghy contains a dead man and a baby girl who is very much alive. Tom, who is lighthouse keeper for the island, prepares to signal to the mainland to report the incident when Isabel stops him. She persuades him that, as the baby was wrapped in a woman's cardigan, the mother must have tragically drowned and suggests that they wait until morning. Tom uneasily agrees, feeling that he owes Isabel time with a baby. He leaves a blank space in his log book so that the incident can be recorded later.

The narrative skips back in time to 1918. In Sydney, Tom Sherborne signs up to become a relief lighthouse keeper. His first posting is six months at Byron Bay, followed by a period on Maatsuyker, a wild, rainy island south of Tasmania. As he works, he dwells on the things he witnessed and was compelled to do as a soldier during World War I. Although he escaped the war without physical injury, Tom is emotionally scarred. He hopes that the honest hard work and solitude involved in his duties as a lightkeeper will help him come to terms with the past.

In June 1920, Tom signs up for an urgent temporary vacancy on Janus Island – an unpopular post due to its hardship and isolation. Both had proved too much for the previous incumbent who had been sent back to the mainland for six months to reassemble his wits. On the way there, Tom travels on the SS Prometheus where he meets a number of other men who served in the war. When Tom discovers one of the men inflicting unwanted attentions on a lady passenger, he intervenes. After reprimanding the man, he informs the lady that she is entitled to report the incident, but points out that her unwanted admirer has undoubtedly been morally damaged by his experiences of war.

Tom arrives in Point Partaguese, the small coastal town from which he will travel to Janus Island. When he lands, a young woman feeding seagulls catches his eye. Her fun-loving, carefree manner is infectious and Tom accepts her invitation to join her in feeding the birds. He stays in a boarding house and in the evening goes for dinner with the Harbourmaster and his wife. At the gathering, he again meets the 'seagull girl,' Isabel Graysmark, along with her parents Bill and Violet. The next day, Tom travels to Janus Island on the store boat, skippered by Ralph Addicott. After a tour around the lighthouse, he is left alone. Tom explores the island and immerses himself in the routines of a lighthouse keeper, taking pride in his work and finding a certain reassurance in it.

Three months later, when the store boat arrives, it brings a light-hearted letter from Isabel Graysmark. Tom pens a quick reply for Ralph to take back to Partaguese.

At the end of his six month contract, Tom returns to Partaguese to find that the previous lightkeeper has lost his wits completely and died jumping off a cliff. Tom agrees to take on the position permanently.

At Isabel's instigation, she and Tom start seeing each other regularly while he is staying in Partaguese. Although he cares for Isabel, he is reluctant to give away details about his family life, other than that his mother is dead and that he is not in touch with his father. Isabel's persistent questioning brings back painful memories for Tom, whose mother left home when he was eight years old. As Tom is due to return to Janus, Isabel proposes to Tom, declaring she wants to live on the island with him as his wife.

After a further six months on the island, Tom returns to Partaguese to marry Isabel. They return to Janus and live happily together. Isabel is delighted when she becomes pregnant but has a miscarriage. She refuses any medical examination afterwards.

PART II

The narrative returns to 27th April 1926 – the day of the arrival of the baby on the island. Isabel begins breastfeeding the baby and calls her Lucy. Tom is alarmed at these developments but sees that his wife is happy for the first time since losing her own babies. The following morning, as Tom prepares to send a signal to the mainland, Isabel suggests that, as no one yet knows that their last baby was stillborn two weeks earlier, they could pretend that 'Lucy' is their own child. Tom is horrified at the suggestion but also recognises that Isabel's mental wellbeing rests on his decision.

Tom buries the body of the dead man on the island and pushes his boat back out to sea. As he does so, he finds a silver rattle in the dinghy. He sends a signal to the mainland communicating the news that their baby has been born. In the weeks that follow, Isabel is joyful and the baby appears to thrive. Tom also begins to fall in love with the baby but remains uneasy over their actions.

In the winter of 1927, Tom's second three-year contract as lightkeeper comes to an end. He, Isabel and Lucy travel to Partaguese for the first time as a family. Isabel's parents fall in love with their new granddaughter, now two years old, and her presence alleviates some of their deeply felt grief over the death of their sons in the war. Her parents' joy only confirms to Isabel that she has made the correct decision in keeping Lucy.

After consulting a doctor, Isabel is shocked to discover that she is experiencing an early menopause and will not be able to have any further children. A christening has been arranged for Lucy, but just before the ceremony, Isabel and Tom see a recently erected memorial for a drowned father and his baby. The father is named as Franz Johannes Roennfeldt and the baby as Grace Ellen. They learn that, on Anzac Day in April 1926, there was an incident which led to Franz (or Frank, as he was known), leaping into a boat with his baby. The 'misunderstanding' clearly involved anti-German feeling and a hostile mob which chased both Frank and his wife, Hannah. As Frank was known to be a poor sailor and also suffered from a weak heart, it was assumed after their disappearance that both father and baby had drowned. The mother of the baby, Hannah Roennfeldt, still lives in Partaguese but has never recovered from the loss. In light of this news, Tom urges Isabel to bring a halt to the christening and insists that they must confess. Once again, Isabel uses delaying tactics and the christening goes ahead. She tells Tom they need time to think and should decide what to do when they return to Janus. Tom's decision is made harder when he overhears Bill and Violet discussing how the birth of Lucy has eased their grief.

As Tom, Isabel and Lucy return to Janus Island, Hannah Roennfeldt receives an anonymous letter. It tells her that her daughter is safe and her husband is at peace. She takes it to the police, but the letter is dismissed as a cruel hoax. Hannah's wealthy father, Septimus Potts, doubles the reward money he is offering for information.

Isabel happily resumes her life on Janus, growing ever closer to Lucy. Although she prays for Hannah, the existence of the child's mother does not seem fully real to her and cannot compete with the intensity of Lucy's physical presence. Distance has grown between Tom and Isabel. Tom is torn between his love for his wife and Lucy and his knowledge that they are depriving another woman of her child.

Tom receives a letter from his father's solicitors informing him that his father died of throat cancer in January 1929. Also enclosed is a letter to Tom from his father written in 1915 along with his mother's locket. The letter explains that Tom's mother wanted him to have the locket when she left but his father felt it was better for his son not to be reminded of her. Tom's father also expresses a wish for reconciliation with him. After reading the letter, Tom feels more understanding towards his father and realises that his mother loved him.

While exploring the island with Lucy, Tom is shocked to discover the little girl unwittingly sitting on her father's grave. The incident brings home to Tom the enormity of burying Frank in an unmarked grave without proper ritual. He tries to convince Isabel that they must tell Hannah the truth, but she refuses.

Tom is granted exceptional shore leave for the 40th anniversary of Janus Lighthouse. During the celebration in Partaguese, he is approached by the woman whose assistance he came to on SS Prometheus years before. She thanks him for his kindness that day and shortly afterwards, Tom realises that the woman is Hannah Roennfeldt. Later, Isabel and Lucy are also introduced to Hannah. Isabel is shaken by encountering Hannah in the flesh and is further disturbed by the fact that Tom has already met her. While Tom and Isabel argue again over whether they should tell Hannah, Lucy goes missing. Tom finds her in a clearing innocently playing with scorpions. Luckily she has not been stung.

Hannah receives a second anonymous letter saying her child is safe and loved. This time, the package also includes the baby's silver rattle. Hannah goes to the police again and a photograph of the rattle is displayed, requesting anyone who recognises it to come forward. Bluey, Ralph's assistant on the store boat, recognises the rattle from his trips to Janus. He confides in his mother, who convinces him that the three thousand guinea reward money will win him back the affections of his beloved, Kitty Kelly.

After only one week back on Janus Island, the Sherbournes are surprised to see the store ship arrive. Accompanying Ralph are four policemen. The policemen question Tom first, who admits to unlawfully keeping the baby, but he insists that he forced Isabel to go along with the deception. Before he is arrested, he promises Isabel he will protect her, as married women cannot be held criminally responsible for anything their husbands force them to do. When Isabel is questioned, she does not contradict Tom's story as she wants to punish him for sending the anonymous letters to Hannah. The police dig up Frank's body and they all return to Partaguese.

PART III

Tom is forced to say a hurried and distressing goodbye to Lucy before he is taken away to the cells. He is to be held at Partaguese police station until his committal hearing, after which he will be transferred to Albany. Isabel becomes hysterical and faints when Lucy is taken away from her to be reunited with her real mother. Sergeant Knuckey, who has known the Graysmark family for years, allows Isabel's father to take his daughter home. Isabel remains determined to punish Tom for his actions.

Hannah's joyful fantasies of a happy reunion with her daughter are quickly shattered. Her daughter refuses to answer to the name Grace and resists Hannah's attempts to bond with her. The little girl cannot understand why Hannah is claiming to be her mother and cries for her real 'Mamma.'

Isabel is questioned by the police again, and by refusing to contradict or confirm their assertions, allows them to believe that Tom bullied her. By choosing not to confirm that Frank was dead when he arrived on Janus, she fuels police suspicions that Tom may have murdered him. Sergeant Knuckey assures Isabel that she will not be punished for her husband's crimes.

Ralph visits Tom in the cells and makes it clear he does not believe that it was Tom's idea to keep the baby. He offers to get him a good lawyer and tries to persuade Tom to tell the truth about Isabel's part in the crime. Tom's lawyer also tries to impress upon Tom the gravity of the situation. He explains that if the courts believe Tom is capable of bullying his wife, they may also believe that he murdered Frank. Tom refuses to be swayed, insisting that he owes it to Isabel to protect her. He is then interrogated by Sergeant Spragg from Albany who is intent upon proving that Tom murdered Frank.

Hannah and her daughter remain desperately unhappy, as the little girl continues to pine for the woman she believes is her mother. Hannah consults the doctor, who insists that Grace must be kept away from Isabel if she is to stand any chance of settling.

Bluey visits Tom at the police station. He tells Tom that he regrets informing the police about the rattle and asks if there is anything he can do to help. Tom asks Bluey to visit Isabel and tell her that he understands. Bluey delivers Tom's message but Isabel sends him away without a reply.

Hannah's sister, Gwen, suggests that it may help Grace to adjust if she sees Isabel, but Hannah will not consider the idea. Hannah's father, Septimus, takes Grace on an outing to see the forest and timber mills he owns. The day is a success and Grace appears to show some signs of settling. She begins to regress again, however, after Hannah and Grace unexpectedly encounter Isabel in the Haberdashers' store. Grace clings to Isabel when she sees her and has to be physically wrenched away.

Gwen, who is living with Hannah and Grace, feels great sympathy for her sister, but cannot bear to witness the little girl's suffering. She takes Grace out for a walk, deliberately leading her through the park where she knows Isabel always sits. Grace and Isabel are overjoyed to see one another and Gwen allows them to spend some time together. When they leave, Gwen tells Isabel that she will try to repeat the exercise and swears both Isabel and Grace to secrecy. In desperation, Hannah visits the doctor again and asks whether it may help Grace if she encourages her to talk about her life on Janus Island. The doctor remains adamant that any mention of the child's old life should be avoided.

Unobserved, Hannah watches Grace playing with her dolls and is shocked to see her re-enact her secret meeting in the park with Isabel. She angrily confronts Gwen who explains that she cannot bear to see how much Grace and Hannah are suffering. She suggests that her sister should give Grace back to Isabel, for her own sake as well as the child's. Hannah vows that Grace will never see Isabel again.

Tom asks Sergeant Knuckey if he can write to Isabel and the policeman reluctantly agrees. Knuckey delivers the letter personally and tells Isabel that Tom needs her help. Isabel begins to open the letter but then puts it away in a drawer, unread.

Hannah visits Tom at the police station and asks him whether he was really solely responsible for the theft of her baby. She wants to understand his motivations but Tom cannot offer her any explanation without betraying Isabel.

Isabel spies on Grace as she plays in Hannah's garden and considers trying to escape with her. Shortly afterwards, Constable Garston calls at the Graysmark's home to report Grace's disappearance. Grace has not been abducted, but has gone in search of Isabel and Tom in the hope that they can all return to Janus Island. As Hannah waits for news of her daughter, she prays and makes a silent pact with God. Later, Sergeant Knuckey finds Grace unharmed, asleep on the Point, and returns her to Hannah.

Isabel visits Ralph and confesses that it was her idea to keep the baby when she arrived on Janus. She is torn between doing the right thing by Tom and the belief that Lucy still needs her. Ralph reminds Isabel of how much Tom loves her and encourages her to admit her role to the police.

Just as Isabel is about to leave her parents' house for the police station, Hannah unexpectedly pays a visit. Hannah explains that Grace's disappearance made her realise that she cannot put her own happiness above her daughter's. She says that if Isabel swears the abduction was all Tom's idea and gives evidence against him, she will let her have Grace. Isabel immediately swears that it was all Tom's doing. When Hannah has gone, Isabel finally reads Tom's letter to her. In it he apologises for hurting her and reiterates his love for her. He declares that the time they spent together was worth what faces him and that he will accept whatever decision she makes.

A storm hits Partaguese and rainwater pours into the ramshackle police station through the back of the building. Sergeant Knuckey is forced to move Tom out of his cell and handcuffs him to an exposed pipe at the front of the police station. Isabel enters the police station but turns to flee when she sees Tom. In desperation, Tom wrenches the pipe from the wall to free himself and embraces her. Isabel begins to confess to Sergeant Knuckey, while Tom tries to stop her.

Sergeant Knuckey visits Hannah to inform her of Isabel's confession. He explains that she will now face trial alongside her husband and that they will go to prison for the rest of their lives. The Sergeant speaks up for Tom and Isabel's good characters and suggests that Hannah could ask for clemency in their case. Furious, Hannah throws a vase at him. After he has left, however, she reflects on her dead husband's forgiving nature and considers what he would do in the circumstances.

Grace goes on another outing with her grandfather, who suggests they could compromise over her name and call her Lucy-Grace. When she returns, she appears happier and more receptive to Hannah. As Hannah teaches her daughter how to make a daisy chain, she experiences a huge sense of relief.

Six months later, Tom and Hannah meet on the jetty at Partaguese. We learn that Tom has spent three months in Bunbury gaol and Isabel received a suspended sentence. They now live in Albany. Tom apologises to Hannah for everything and thanks her for contributing to their light sentences by speaking in their defence at the trial. Hannah says that, although she doesn't forgive them, she wants to move on without dwelling on the past. Tom assures Hannah that they will never contact Lucy-Grace again, but asks if one day she could tell her daughter that they loved her. Hannah returns home where her daughter happily greets her as 'mummy.'

Tom visits Isabel in the nursing home in Albany where she is recuperating. Isabel cannot understand why Tom finds it so easy to forgive her and insists that everything is ruined. Tom declares that they belong together.

The story moves forward to August 1950 and the setting is Hopetoun, nearly 400 miles from Partaguese. We learn that Tom and Isabel bought a farm here following the trial. They lived a quiet life, with occasional visits from Isabel's parents, who have now died. Tom still writes to Ralph, who now lives with his daughter and family after the death of his wife. Tom and Isabel never returned to Partaguese. They were married for 30 years before Isabel died of cancer.

A woman arrives at Tom's farm with a baby and introduces herself as Lucy-Grace Rutherford (née Roennfeldt). She explains that she had discovered that Isabel was terminally ill and her mother had given her blessing to visit. Tom sadly informs Lucy-Grace that Isabel died a week previously.

Lucy-Grace tells Tom that she moved to Perth with her mother when she was five to make a new start. Hannah moved back to Partaguese in 1944, however, when Lucy-Grace joined the WAAF and has settled there with her sister, Gwen. Lucy-Grace met her husband while they were both in the air force. She explains to Tom that she often thought about her 'other parents' over the years, but couldn't understand their actions until she had her own son, Christopher. Tom gives Lucy-Grace a letter which Isabel left for her in case she ever sought them out. The letter asks Lucy-Grace's forgiveness. Tom also gives her a chest containing keepsakes from her childhood. Lucy-Grace thanks Tom for saving her and taking such good care of her. When she leaves, she chooses to leave the chest with Tom, implying that she will return to visit him again.

9 - CHARACTER ANALYSIS

One of the great strengths of this novel is the author's vivid portrayal of sympathetic yet flawed characters. The majority of its cast are 'good people' who, faced with difficult choices, do not always take the moral highroad. Stedman beautifully depicts the inner workings of her characters' minds as they wrestle between what their heart desires and what they know to be right.

Tom Sherbourne

Tom is in his late twenties at the start of the novel. Although he has been awarded the Military Cross for bravery during World War I, he denies that he is a war hero, as the depravities of war have left him deeply traumatised. He is also haunted by the loss of his mother when he was eight years old. His father's refusal to allow Tom contact with her after she leaves is further complicated by Tom's belief that it was his fault that his father found out about her affair. The decisions Tom's father makes in the 'best interests' of his son have striking parallels with the decisions that are made by Isabel and Hannah over the future of Lucy-Grace.

Honourable and trustworthy, Tom is the moral lynchpin of the novel. His instincts are unerringly to do good and hurt no one. The role of lighthouse keeper offers him the opportunity to save lives rather than take him and promises the solitude he craves. Conflict arises for Tom when he is made to compromise his moral integrity - first during the war when he has to kill other men and then again when he tries to make Isabel happy. Although Tom is a man of few words and at times seems emotionally restrained, his unwavering love for Isabel is one of the most moving aspects of the novel. He is torn between the knowledge that, without a child his love alone is not enough for Isabel and the certainty that they are committing an unforgivable sin in keeping a baby that does not belong to them. Isabel encourages Tom to ignore the voice of his conscience, but he is constantly troubled by it, finally leading him to actions which give away their crime.

Tom feels a mixture of grief and relief when he is arrested as he cannot live with the knowledge that they are depriving another woman of her child. He also feels that there is a certain justice in whatever fate awaits him as he believes there should be a price to pay for the lives he took during the war. The burden of guilt that Tom willingly carries makes him an easy scapegoat for both Isabel's wrath and Sergeant Spragg's determination to convict him.

Isabel Sherbourne née Graysmark

Isabel is only 19 years old when she first meets Tom. She has led a sheltered life in Point Partaguese, marred only by the death of her brothers in the war. Tom is attracted by her lively, fun-loving nature and youthful optimism. In the early stages of their relationship, Isabel is undoubtedly a positive influence on Tom, coaxing him out of his reclusive shell with her spontaneity and love. When Isabel is confronted with the realisation that she may never be a mother, however, she sinks into depression and changes beyond recognition. Whilst Tom is stoic in the face of suffering, Isabel is unable to accept it. Tom compares her personality to the properties of mercury, having the ability to 'cure' but also to 'poison.'

At times, Isabel's actions are shockingly selfish. She places her own happiness above the suffering of Lucy's real mother, shows herself to be an adept liar and shamelessly manipulates Tom in order to keep the baby. Until very late in the novel, Isabel rarely questions whether her own actions are right, focusing all of her pain and frustration on Tom, whom she almost allows to be wrongly tried for murder. On the other hand, while Lucy is in her care, Isabel shows herself to be a natural and loving mother. It is this maternal instinct, left cruelly unsatisfied by nature, which drives her to behave in the way that she does.

Lucy Sherbourne/Grace Roennfeldt

Throughout the novel, the identity of Lucy/Grace is forever shifting. She is by turns, Grace, Lucy, Grace again and finally Lucy-Grace. She washes up on Janus Island as Grace Roennfeldt and is transformed into Lucy Sherbourne or 'Lulu Lighthouse,' as she calls herself. For the first few years of her life, the isolation of Janus Island provides a misleadingly safe and reassuring sense of identity for Lucy. Isabel, Tom and the island become her entire world and she has no concept of anything beyond it.

Although Lucy has occasional trips to the 'real' world from the age of two, her experiences remain very limited, as is demonstrated when she is found innocently playing with scorpions. While she understands the nature of her world on Janus, including its dangers, everything beyond it is a mystery.

Lucy's transformation back to Grace Roennfeldt is a sudden and shocking one. When Tom is arrested and she is taken back to Partaguese permanently, she is presented with a new home and mother with very little explanation as to why. Her new mother's insistence on calling her Grace underlines the fact that she cannot even be sure of who she is any more. The claims of both Isabel and Hannah that they are her mother add to her distress and sense of confusion. She pines for Isabel and Tom, but quickly begins to internalise these feelings as she realises that mention of her old life makes her new mother unhappy. One of the most poignant moments of the novel is Grace's reaction when Hannah catches her re-enacting her secret meetings with Isabel in the park. Before Hannah can speak, Grace anticipates her mother's anger and smacks her own hand calling herself 'Bad Lucy!'

When Lucy-Grace reappears at the end of the novel it is as Lucy-Grace Rutherford, a married woman and a mother in her own right. She explains to Tom that she and her mother moved to Perth when she was five years old for a new start. Lucy-Grace's acknowledgement of the contributions that both the Sherbournes and Hannah made towards her life is an important one. The memories she still has of Janus Island and her love of the ocean are as much a part of her as the life she has spent with Hannah. Her desire to contact Tom and Isabel and thank them demonstrates that, despite the traumatic events of the past, she sees something positive in their involvement with her life. The birth of her own child has led her to understand the fierce maternal bond that led both Isabel and Hannah to behave in the way they did.

Hannah Roennfeldt née Potts

As the daughter of the rich timber merchant, Septimus Potts, Hannah led a privileged childhood, overshadowed by the death of her mother. Educated at an expensive boarding school, she went on to do a degree – a significant achievement for a woman at the time.

When Hannah falls in love with Frank, it demonstrates an admirable disregard for both social standing and public opinion. Tired of being chased by suitors attracted by her father's money, Hannah immediately falls for Frank's goodness of heart. She is unconcerned by Frank's meagre income and despises the xenophobic attitudes of local people towards him. When her father cuts her off for marrying 'a Hun,' they live happily in a rundown cottage in conditions far beneath what Hannah has been used to.

When Frank and Grace disappear, we learn that Hannah's grief drives her dangerously close to a breakdown. Ironically, however, when Grace is miraculously returned to her, after her initial joy, Hannah experiences a despair which is almost worse than her original period of mourning. Her daughter returns in body only, as in all other respects she is a hostile stranger. Hannah vacillates between despair and anger as her attempts to bond with Grace fall on stony ground and she is forced to confront exactly what the Sherbournes have stolen from her.

Hannah is very different in character to Isabel and this is demonstrated in their respective relationships with Lucy-Grace. Whilst Isabel is warm and very physically affectionate with the little girl, Hannah is naturally more restrained, which, at times, makes her appear rather cold in comparison. Hannah, however, is far more inclined to examine her own emotions and motivations and to consider what is 'right.' Whilst Isabel is driven purely by her desire to mother Lucy, no matter what the consequences, Hannah agonises over what is the best course of action for her daughter. Whilst both women turn their anger against Tom, Hannah is continually plagued by her instinct that he is a good man (formed by her encounter with him on the ship). Hannah's painful decision to return Grace to Isabel demonstrates that ultimately she is prepared to place her daughter's well-being above her own.

When Hannah speaks up for Isabel and Tom during their trial, she is acknowledging the pointlessness of bitterness and rage. Her ability to let go of the past is also demonstrated when she gives Lucy-Grace her blessing to visit the Sherbournes.

Septimus Potts

Hannah's father, Septimus, is a complex character - both deeply flawed and sympathetic. Although he is a wealthy timber merchant, his origins could not be more humble. The seventh child of a poor English family, he was sent over to Australia as a five-year-old in the hope that a decent family would take him in.

Septimus is a good father to his two daughters after his beloved wife dies, doing his best to make up for the absence of their mother. When Hannah meets Frank, however, he displays an unsympathetic and racist streak when he cuts his daughter off for marrying a man who is 'practically

German.' When Grace is returned to Hannah, he sees it as an opportunity to redeem himself for his past failings. Septimus feels great sympathy for his daughter's pain as she fails to bond with Grace but also shows touching understanding of how the child must be feeling. He explains to her that he too had to start again with a new family when he was a child and emphasises some of the positive outcomes of this experience. Septimus takes the time to introduce the little girl to some of the wonders of her new environment on their days out. He is also the first to suggest the concession of calling her Lucy-Grace, recognising that her previous life cannot simply be erased.

Gwen Potts

Gwen is Hannah's younger sister. She supports Hannah through her grief when Frank and Grace disappear, and then again through her despair when Grace is returned to her. Gwen is fair-minded and tries to view her sister's situation objectively. Although she understands why Hannah does not want Grace to see Isabel, she is painfully aware that both her sister and Grace are desperately unhappy. After failing to persuade Hannah to let Grace have contact with Isabel, Gwen takes the situation into her own hands and arranges clandestine meetings in the park. When Hannah discovers this betrayal, Gwen suggests that Hannah should give Grace back to Isabel for the sake of her own sanity.

Franz/ Frank Roennfeldt

Frank is of course the body in the boat at the beginning of the novel. He is also Grace's real father and Hannah's husband. It is his persecution by the residents of Partaguese that begins the dramatic chain of events in the novel.

Although Frank is a humble baker when Hannah meets and falls in love with him, he stems from a privileged Austrian family. Due to his father's debts, he moved to Australia as a child along with his father, who promptly threw himself under a train. Frank makes a life for himself working in his uncle's and aunt's bakery and changing his name from Franz to Frank in order to fit in with Australian society.

Frank's persecution as an 'almost German' is ironic as he took no part in the war. On Anzac Day he becomes a scapegoat for the locals' unresolved grief and anger over the loved ones they have lost. He jumps into the boat to keep his baby safe from the drunken mob but presumably becomes a victim of rough seas and a weak heart. Despite the racism he endured, we learn that Frank had a forgiving nature and did not believe in bitterness or resentment. When Hannah agonises over whether to punish the Sherbournes for their actions, she eventually chooses the path she knows her husband would have taken.

Violet Graysmark

Isabel's mother, Violet, has herself experienced the pain of losing children. Both of her sons are killed during World War I and she takes solace in the arrival of her granddaughter, Lucy. Violet understands her daughter's desperation for a child and never condemns her actions.

Bill Graysmark

As headmaster of the school in Point Partaguese, Isabel's father is a pillar of the community and generally a good judge of character. When Tom is arrested, instinct tells Bill that his son-in-law is neither a bully nor a murderer. Bill's protective paternal love outweighs what he knows in his heart to be true, however, and he supports his daughter until she confesses.

Alfie and Hugh Graysmark

The sons of Bill and Violet, and Isabel's brothers. They both die in the Somme.

Ralph Addicott

Ralph is the experienced skipper of the store boat, 'The Windward Spirit,' which delivers supplies to Janus Island every three months. During his visits to Janus, Ralph comes to respect Tom for his integrity and he never believes for a moment that Tom is guilty of the crimes he is accused of. Ralph visits Tom in the cells and tries to persuade him to admit Isabel's part in events. He also tries to persuade Isabel that Tom does not deserve to suffer.

Hilda Addicott

Ralph's wife.

Bluey Smart

Bluey is Ralph's naïve young assistant on 'The Windward Spirit.' He becomes the unlikely downfall of the Sherbournes when he recognises the photograph of the silver rattle. Persuaded by his mother to report what he knows, he later bitterly regrets his actions and refuses to accept the reward money.

Sergeant Knuckey

The senior police officer of Point Partaguese, Sergeant Knuckey is a sympathetic character. One of his own children, Billy, died when he was young and although their five other children survived, his wife never fully recovered. Like Tom, he has also seen horrors in the war that he does not like to dwell on. His own experiences lend him a compassion for all the parties involved in the 'theft' of Grace and he is determined to be fair and thorough in dealing with it.

It is thanks to Sergeant Knuckey that Tom is held in Partaguese rather than being directly transferred to Albany for trial, which doubtless saves him from being falsely convicted of Frank's murder. It is also his conversation with Hannah that persuades her to speak up for Isabel and Tom during the trial.

Sergeant Spragg

Spragg is the ambitious police officer from Albany who likes to throw his weight about. A stickler for the rulebook, he is an example of how rules and regulations can be dangerous if they are exercised without compassion. As he did not serve in the war, Spragg has a chip on his shoulder about all those who did and takes an immediate dislike to Tom when he learns he is a war hero. His determination to prove that Tom murdered Frank is thankfully foiled by Sergeant Knuckey's more humane approach to law and order.

Constable Garstone

Garstone is the young officer stationed at Partaguese police station. He is also part of the mob which chases Frank on Anzac Day.

Trimble Docherty

Trimble is the unfortunate keeper of Janus Light before Tom. He was removed from his position for a period of recuperation after reporting that his recently deceased wife was signalling to passing ships. He later dies, jumping off a cliff, believing that he is boarding a boat skippered by his wife. His story serves as a warning of the effects of grief and isolation.

Neville Whittnish

Neville temporarily takes over as keeper of Janus Light before Tom takes up the role and then again, when Tom is arrested. Despite his grumpy disposition, Neville cannot help but be impressed by Tom's meticulous care of the lighthouse. As a mark of respect, when the police arrive on Janus to take Tom away, Neville ensures Tom has opportunity to say goodbye to the lighthouse.

Captain Percy Hasluck and Mrs Hasluck

The Harbourmaster of Point Partaguese and his wife. When Tom is invited to dinner with them, he meets Isabel for the second time.

Cyril Chipper and Bertha Chipper

Chairman of the local Roads Board and his wife.

Gerald Fitzgerald

Tom's lawyer.

Mrs Mewett

Owner of the boarding house where Tom stays in Partaguese.

Mrs Inkpen

The hard-faced woman who takes over the farriers in Partaguese when her husband fails to return from Gallipoli.

10 - QUESTIONS FOR DISCUSSION

1/ Tom is haunted by his experiences during World War I. In what way does this impact on his decisions and actions throughout the novel?

2/ Tom believes that keeping to the rules prevents men from becoming savages. Do you agree, or is Isabel right to think that love is more important?

3/ Isabel sees the arrival of the baby on the island as a gift from God and several of the other characters try to converse with God through prayer. Discuss the role of faith in the novel.

4/ Do you think Isabel would have come to terms with her childlessness if an apparently motherless baby hadn't been thrown in her path? Does living on Janus Island intensify her craving for children?

5/ Does Isabel have any right to think of herself as Lucy's mother?

6/ Which character's perspective did you most sympathise with and why? Did your sympathies alter as the novel progressed?

7/ The beam of Janus lighthouse illuminates the ocean for miles around, but leaves the island itself in darkness. Discuss the effects of isolation on Tom and Isabel. In what respects does it lead them into a moral darkness?

8/ Hannah has experienced a great deal more loss in her life than Isabel (her mother, her husband and her daughter). Do you think Isabel's grief for her dead babies is in any way comparable?

9/ Is Tom's love for Isabel greater than her love for him? Will the pull of maternal love always be more powerful than that of romantic love?

10/ Discuss how Frank becomes the scapegoat for the grief and loss the residents of Partaguese feel after the war. In what way does Tom also become a scapegoat for the buried emotions of the other characters?

11/ Do you think Hannah could have handled Grace's transition back into her old life better? Is she right to refuse contact between Grace and Isabel?

12/ What do you believe finally prompts Isabel's decision to confess at the police station? Did her decision surprise you?

13/ Which family do you believe Lucy-Grace should have stayed with? Can you think of any other ways in which the situation could have been resolved?

14/ The redemptive power of forgiveness is an important theme in the novel. Discuss how the major characters feel about forgiveness and why.

15/ Do you think the novel implies that doing the right thing is more important than personal happiness? Is it possible to be truly happy if it is at the expense of someone else's grief?

11 - QUICK QUIZ

Questions

How many of the following trivia questions can you answer correctly? Answers can be found on page 39:-

Q1/ What is Janus the god of?

Q2/ What is Isabel doing when Tom first sees her?

Q3/ What does Isabel do to Tom's map of Janus Island?

Q4/ Apart from a baby and a dead man, what other two objects are in the dinghy that lands on Janus Island?

Q5/ What is Lucy doing on the only occasion when Tom tells her off?

Q6/ What nationality is Frank and what is his real name?

Q7/ Why is Hannah's father, Septimus, sent alone to Australia when he is just a small boy?

Q8/ How often does the store boat visit Janus Island?

Q9/ What does Tom's father enclose in his final letter to his son?

Q10/ When Hannah prays in church, whose statue does she sit by?

Q11/ Lucy/ Grace goes missing on two occasions. In each instance, where is she eventually found and what is she doing?

Q12/ After Isabel has her first miscarriage, who does Tom bring to Janus in an attempt to lift his wife's spirits?

Q13/ How does Trimble Docherty, the previous lightkeeper of Janus, die?

Q14/ Where does Lucy-Grace meet her husband?

Q15/ Why does Lucy-Grace leave the chest of childhood keepsakes with Tom?

Answers

A1/ Doorways

A2/ Feeding the seagulls

A3/ Annotates it with her own place names

A4/ A woman's cardigan and a silver rattle

A5/ Sitting on her father's unmarked grave

A6/ Austrian – Franz

A7/ His mother is dying of consumption and she hopes he will find a family to take care of him there

A8/ Every three months

A9/ His mother's locket

A10/ Saint Jude – the patron saint of desperate causes

A11/ She is found in a clearing playing with scorpions and then asleep on the Point

A12/ A piano restorer

A13/ He jumps off a cliff believing he is boarding a boat skippered by his dead wife

A14/ They are both in the air force

A15/ So that she will have a reason to visit him again

12 - FURTHER READING

Lighthouse Themed

To the Lighthouse, Virginia Woolf (1927)

The Blackwater Lightship, Colm Tóibín (1999)

The Lighthouse, Alison Moore (2012)

Novels Centred Around Lies or Deception

Atonement, Ian McEwan (2001)

The Husband's Secret, Liane Moriarty (2013)

The Cry, Helen FitzGerald (2013)

Necessary Lies, Diane Chamberlain (2013)

The Lie, Helen Dunmore (2014)

Mother / Child Relationships

The Hand that First Held Mine, Maggie O'Farrell (2010)

The Snow Child, Eowyn Ivey (2012)

Between a Mother and Her Child, Elisabeth Noble (2012)

Australian Historical Fiction

Remembering Babylon, David Malouf (1994)

True History of the Kelly Gang, Peter Carey (2000)

The Secret River, Kate Grenville (2006)

The Narrow Road to the Deep North, Richard Flanagan (2014)

Shame and the Captives, Thomas Keneally (2014)

Further Titles in The Reading Room series

Frankenstein: A Guide for Book Clubs

Gone Girl: A Guide for Book Clubs

The Book Thief: A Guide for Book Clubs

The Fault in Our Stars: A Guide for Book Clubs

The Great Gatsby: A Guide for Book Clubs

The Goldfinch: A Guide for Book Clubs

The Guernsey Literary and Potato Peel Pie Society: A Guide for Book Clubs

The Husband's Secret: A Guide for Book Clubs

The Light Between Oceans: A Guide for Book Clubs

The Storied Life of A.J. Fikry: A Guide for Book Clubs

BIBLIOGRAPHY

Andrews, Eric. *The Anzac Illusion: Anglo-Australian Relations during World War I*, Cambridge University Press, 1993

Knightley, Phillip. *Australia: A Biography of a Nation*, Vintage, 2001

Stedman, M.L. *The Light Between Oceans*, Random House, 2012

ABOUT THE AUTHOR

Kathryn Cope graduated in English Literature from Manchester University and obtained her masters from The University of York. She is a reviewer and author of The Reading Room Book Group Guides. She lives in the English Peak District with her husband and son. The Reading Room series covers a wide range of titles for book group discussion from F. Scott Fitzgerald's classic *The Great Gatsby* to Gillian Flynn's contemporary bestseller, *Gone Girl.*

Made in the USA
Middletown, DE
23 October 2017